SPORTS' TOP MVPS™

DISCARD

KOBE BRYANT

XINA M. UHL

rosen publishing's
rosen
central®

New York

To Daniel and Luke, basketballers in training

Published in 2019 by The Rosen Publishing Group, Inc.
29 East 21st Street, New York, NY 10010

Library of Congress Cataloging-in-Publication Data

Names: Uhl, Xina M., author. Title: Kobe Bryant / Xina M. Uhl.
Description: New York : Rosen Publishing, 2019. | Series: Sports' Top MVPs | Includes
bibliographical references and index. | Audience: Grades: 5–8.
Identifiers: LCCN 2017044965| ISBN 9781508181989 (library bound) | ISBN
9781508181996 (paperback).
Subjects: LCSH: Bryant, Kobe, 1978– —Juvenile literature. | Basketball players—
United States—Biography—Juvenile literature. | Los Angeles Lakers (Basketball
team)—History—Juvenile literature.
Classification: LCC GV884.B794 U55 2019 | DDC 796.323092 [B] —dc23LC record
available at https://lccn.loc.gov/2017044965

Manufactured in the United States of America

On the cover: Kobe Bryant drives in to score against the Utah Jazz at the Staples
Center on April 13, 2016, in Los Angeles, California.

12/11/18   23.85

CONTENTS

January 22, 2006, Los Angeles Staples Center. Less than a minute remained in the square-off between the Los Angeles Lakers and the Toronto Raptors. Laker Kobe Bryant stepped to the free throw line, gripping the basketball between his hands. He looked at the basket and took a deep breath. Then he shot—and made the basket.

"An 81-point game!" the announcer cried. "Ladies and gentlemen, you have witnessed the second-greatest scoring performance in NBA history!"

From the stands, the crowd chanted, "MVP! MVP!"

Bryant's shot gave the Lakers the game, 122–104. But Bryant himself scored a record eighty-one of those points, the best of his career—and second only to Wilt Chamberlain's 1962 one-hundred-point game. The Lakers had been down by eighteen points in the third quarter, but then Bryant took over, scoring an incredible fifty-five points in the second half of the game. He'd shot 28–46 from the field and 7–13 from the three-point line, and he made eighteen of twenty free throws. There was no doubt about it. Kobe Bryant had hit the high point in his career. He had become a basketball legend.

Drafted by the National Basketball Association (NBA) right out of high school, he was quickly traded to the Los Angeles Lakers, where he spent his entire twenty-year-long career. Bryant made a splash before his professional basketball career had even begun, with the media proclaiming him the next big thing. They turned out to be right, because he became the NBA's youngest-ever star when he was selected to play in an All-Star Game in his second season.

Bryant made history as both one of the NBA's highest scorers and the youngest all-star player. With his help, the

Kobe Bryant concentrates as he takes a foul shot during a January 2006 Lakers game against the Indiana Pacers played in Los Angeles.

LA Lakers captured five NBA championships in 2000, 2001, 2002, 2009, and 2010. During the 2005–2006 and 2006–2007 seasons he led the league in scoring. In 2008, he was named MVP for the first time in his career. He would go on to capture the honor twice more.

As a member of the US men's basketball team at the Olympics in Beijing in 2008 and London in 2012, he won gold medals both times. In 2017, after his retirement, he joined the board of directors for Los Angeles' 2024 Olympics bid in order to bring the Olympic Games to the LA area, an effort that succeeded Los Angeles being named host city of the 2028 summer games.

While Bryant is best known for his basketball feats, there's more to him. He's a married father to three children, an enthusiastic advocate of charity work, and even an actor, producer, and writer of television and movies.

Bryant's inborn talent and hard-won skill, combined with his integrity and fierce competitive nature, gave him a special place in the annals of basketball history. Some have even called him the greatest basketball player of all time. He may have retired from the game in 2016, but he's not done living.

CHAPTER ONE

LITTLE BEAN

Kobe Bean Bryant was born on August 23, 1978, in Philadelphia, Pennsylvania. His father is Joe "Jellybean" Bryant, an NBA star for the 76ers, Clippers, and Rockets for eight years. His mother is Pam Bryant, and he has two older sisters, Shaya and Sharia. His unusual first name resulted from his parents naming him after the Kobe Japanese steakhouse in the Philadelphia suburbs. His nickname, Bean, comes from his father's nickname, Jellybean.

Bryant says he first started playing basketball at age three. A few years later, when he was six, his family moved to Italy, where Joe began his European basketball career for another eight years. Bryant learned Italian and began playing sports. He enjoyed soccer so much that he considered making it a career. Instead, he began to play basketball.

His family moved back to the United States when Kobe was thirteen. Now six feet, six inches (1.98 meters) tall, he played basketball in Lower Merion High School in Ardmore, Pennsylvania, a suburb of Philadelphia. Adjusting to life back in the United States was a challenge. Though he spoke English, he did not know the slang other kids spoke.

Kobe Bryant's parents, Joe and Pam Bryant, cheer him on from courtside during Game 2 of the Western Conference semifinals on May 4, 2010. The Lakers triumphed over the Utah Jazz 111–103.

Later in his life, fellow players, sports announcers, and others would speak about his personal qualities of a strong drive, intense competitiveness, and dedication to basketball. Those personal qualities showed up early in his life. Kobe and his dad played one-on-one games where he learned how to act as a professional.

In high school, Kobe showed up for basketball practice at 5:00 am and stayed until 7:00 pm—the beginning of an incredible work ethic that

Kobe Bryant spent his high school years at Lower Merion High School in a well-to-do suburb of Philadelphia, Pennsylvania. He speaks about his time there as fond memories.

he would keep up long after he left high school. He has never made any bones about it—even in high school, basketball was his life and all he ever wanted to do.

By the time Kobe became a senior, he was called the best high school player in the country. Hype followed him around like his shadow. Basketball scouts attended every game, and the national media sent camera crews to hang out in the hallways and even attend his classes.

A SHORT HISTORY OF BASKETBALL

Basketball is defined as a game played between two five-player teams on a rectangular court that can be outdoors or indoors. At each end of the court is an elevated hoop with a net called a basket. Each team's objective is to score points by tossing the ball through the opponent's basket.

The game was invented by James Naismith (1861–1939) on or about December 1, 1891, and it was first played at the International Young Men's Christian Association (YMCA) Training School in Springfield, Massachusetts, where Naismith was a physical education instructor.

As goals, Naismith used two half-bushel peach baskets, giving the sport its name. Enthusiastic students spread the word about the new game. Before long, a number of associations wrote Naismith for a copy of the rules. He published these in the January 15, 1892, issue of the *Triangle*, the YMCA Training School's campus paper.

Early on, the number of players varied depending on how many students were in class and how big the playing area was. In 1894, teams were standardized according to playing area size. When the size is less than 1,800 square feet (167.2 square meters) there are five players; for an area 1,800 to 3,600 square feet (334.5 sq m) there are seven players, and the number rises to nine when the playing area exceeds that.

Naismith and five of the original basketball players were Canadians, and Canada was the first country besides the United States to play the game. It expanded to France in 1893, to England in 1894, to Australia, China, and India soon thereafter, and to Japan in 1900. It remains the only major sport of entirely US origin.

As a professional basketball league, the NBA formed in the United States in 1949. It combined two rival groups: the National Basketball League, founded in 1937, and the Basketball Association of America, founded in 1946. In 1976, the American

Basketball Association (ABA) broke up, and the NBA absorbed four of its teams. The NBA membership includes two conferences, each with three divisions.

The NBA governs the behavior of players, fans, and the league with detailed codes of conduct. It also governs the selection of arenas and the presence of security personnel and sales of food and beverages.

The Women's National Basketball Association (WNBA) was established by the NBA in 1997. While it attracts a small percentage of sports fans as compared to NBA teams, it has become the most successful professional women's sports league in the United States to date.

John Osipowicz, who taught English to Kobe, recalls, "They said to act normal when the cameras were there. But it is a bit hard when you turn around and bump into a camera."

The fame made Kobe bold. At an event put on by the magazine *Essence*, he approached young R&B singer Brandy Norwood. He identified himself as the number one high school basketball player in the world and asked her to attend prom with him. Brandy told entertainment news site Zimbio, "Next thing you know, Kobe flew my mom and I out. Made me feel like a queen. It was like royal treatment and then we went to prom. I just felt like a normal 17-year-old, it was so much fun, although it was cameras and media there, it still felt normal to be in a school with kids my age."

Kobe lived up to the high school hype by leading his school team to capture the Pennsylvania State Championship. His efforts earned him the Naismith Player of the Year. Overall, he led his high school basketball team to state championships four years in a row. While in high school, he

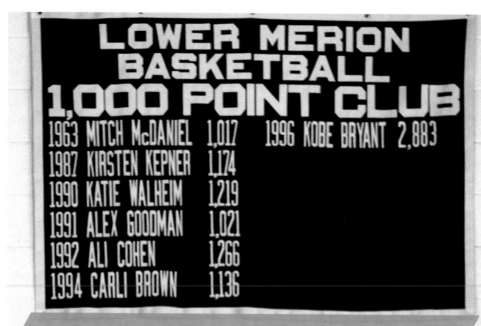

The gym at Lower Merion High School honors its basketball players who have scored more than a thousand points. Bryant's score set a record there and across the state.

also started working out with the Philadelphia 76ers. It was clear that he was destined for great things.

Upon graduation, Kobe had a big decision to make. Should he follow the normal path of future professional NBA athletes and attend college? Or should he take his chances with professional basketball?

CHAPTER TWO

RISING STAR

In 1996, Kobe Bryant graduated from Lower Merion High School. He had already garnered extensive attention as the top-rated high school player in the nation, but there was college to think of. Most professional basketball players go to college first, and Bryant had good grades and high SAT scores, so schoolwork was not a problem. Some coaches believe that joining professional leagues too young is not good for players. Colleges had come to Bryant with multiple offers. These included the University of North Carolina (UNC), Duke University, the University of Kansas (KU), and West Point. Bryant leaned most strongly toward attending UNC.

In the end, Bryant opted to skip college altogether and turn pro immediately. The decision was controversial. Experts claim that most players right out of high school aren't ready for the pressure of professional competition, in mind and body. Later, players Kevin Garnett and LeBron James also succeeded in jumping from high school straight to the NBA. But in 2006, the NBA implemented a rule that players must be out of high school for at least one year before they are eligible to enter the NBA draft. Bryant has no regrets, though. On February 13, 2016, he told USA Today, "The best decision [I ever made was] coming straight to the NBA and skipping college. That's it—the best one."

Bryant shows off his jersey as he stands between Lakers general manager Jerry West and head coach Del Harris. Harris coached Bryant during his first years as a professional basketball star.

In 1996, during the NBA Draft's first round, shooting guard Kobe Bryant was the league's thirteenth draft pick, going to the Charlotte Hornets. Almost immediately, he was traded to the Los Angeles Lakers for Vlade Divac, a center. A Lakers fan since he lived in Italy, the trade pleased Bryant.

If anything, the media frenzy surrounding Bryant increased. At only eighteen years of age, many claimed that he would be the next Michael Jordan. Bryant's qualities as a person impressed sports commentators, coaches, and others. He was hardworking, unbelievably competitive, well spoken, well mannered, and able to handle the press with skill and sophistication. And then there was the way he played basketball, with grace, style, and unquestionable ability.

A ROCKY START

Bryant may not regret skipping college to go pro immediately after high school, but that doesn't mean it was the easiest transition for him or the Lakers. His intense popularity—not to mention the five-year endorsement deal with Adidas he had scored before he even had a chance to play—generated jealousy among some of his teammates. He soon realized that he had nothing in common with his older teammates, many of whom socialized at bars, where Bryant could not legally

Kobe Bryant wears his original number 8 jersey as he steals the ball from the Boston Celtics on December 28, 1997.

drink alcohol. He became a loner, practicing obsessively, and keeping aloof from the other teammates.

On the court, he excelled, just like everyone had hoped. Choosing jersey number 8, rookie shooting guard Bryant did not have the best start to his career. On a visit to Venice Beach, he broke his wrist and consequently missed playing during training camp. In fact, he was not able to play for the Lakers until early November. During that first game, against the Minnesota Timberwolves, Bryant played for only six minutes and scored zero points. Two days later, in a game against the Knicks, he played for only three minutes. At least this time he scored one point, though.

Bryant faced off against childhood idol Michael Jordan of the Chicago Bulls during the NBA All-Star Game on February 8, 1998.

Head coach Del Harris approached Bryant with care, calling him a "teenager in a teenager's body." Bryant worked hard, though. Harris told the *Los Angeles Times*, "As the season went along, he just kept getting better and better. By the end of the year, he was central to the rotation. He was a key player." Despite his status as a key player, he was a reserve player for the first two seasons.

During the 1997–1998 season, Bryant was voted a starter for the 1998 All-Star Game. At nineteen years old, he had become the youngest all-star in NBA history. Lakers teammate center Shaquille O'Neal (known as Shaq) came on board the same season that Bryant did, and the two of them would go on to make Lakers history.

Del Harris was fired in 1999, and Kurt Rambis filled in as coach for the rest of the 1998–1999 season before a new head coach was hired—Phil Jackson. Bryant admits that everything changed when Jackson became coach. Before he came along, Bryant thought about the game from a tactical perspective. But Jackson was big on mindfulness and spirituality, on controlling one's ego, so that Bryant could play basketball effortlessly. That didn't mean that everything was easy between Bryant and Jackson. In fact, Jackson once referred to Bryant as "uncoachable." The source of their conflict lay in the fact that Jackson

PHIL JACKSON, NBA COACH EXTRAORDINAIRE

Praised as one of the greatest coaches in the history of basketball, Phil Jackson has led his teams to a record eleven championships. He was born in Deer Lodge, Montana, on September 17, 1945, the son of evangelical ministers. As a player, he joined the NBA in 1967 and proceeded to garner two championships for the New York Knicks. Though he was a smart, hardworking player, he was never a star.

After he retired as a player in 1980, he took up coaching, starting out his career as an assistant coach for the New Jersey Nets. In the mid-1980s he became head coach of the Albany Patroons. He moved to the Chicago Bulls in 1987 to work as an assistant coach. In 1989, he was promoted to head coach. There, he became known for his use of the triangle offense as well as coaching techniques that made use of Eastern philosophy and Native American spiritual beliefs. He coached star players Michael Jordan, Scottie Pippen, and Dennis Rodman and led the team to six championships in 1991, 1992, 1993, 1996, 1997, 1998.

Jackson moved to the LA Lakers in 1999 and achieved immediate success with three consecutive winning titles from 2000 to 2002. Kobe Bryant and Shaquille O'Neal often clashed, and Bryant regularly ignored Jackson's offense plans. Jackson quit in 2004, then returned as head coach in 2005, where he flourished and was inducted into the Basketball Hall of Fame in 2007.

During the 2008–2009 season, after he led the Lakers to the championship, he earned his tenth NBA title as head coach. After another Laker championship win in 2010, he left the Lakers following the 2011 play-off season. In 2014, he returned to New York to serve a five-year tenure as the president of the New York Knicks.

often pushed Bryant to be more disciplined, while Bryant wanted more freedom.

In fact, Jackson admitted in an interview that quite often he could feel Bryant's hatred when the two disagreed. Despite this friction, the two found a way to work together. But Jackson wasn't the only one to sometimes rub Bryant the wrong way. Shaq did also. But together the two superstar players were to reach the heights of success over the next few years.

CHAPTER THREE

ALL-STAR, SUPERSTAR

Alpha male. The term refers to a dominant male, one who leads because he is the strongest, the fastest, the best competitor in a pack—or on a basketball team. From the time Kobe Bryant and Shaquille O'Neal started playing together on the Lakers, they clashed. Coach Phil Jackson knew the reason: they both were alpha males with big egos.

They were also very different. Shaq was older, more experienced. He had a laid-back, playful personality. Kobe was the young buck, less experienced but confident in his abilities. His personality was intense. He was driven and hardworking.

Rick Fox, a former team member of both men, had this to say to the *Los Angeles Times*: "It's hard to have two alphas, you know? I just think they were in different eras. Shaq was older, Kobe was younger. Shaq was already established and Kobe was trying to establish himself. I think when I look back on it, that was the difference in each of their careers where they were at a different point and different stages where both were really striving to be the best in the game."

Sometimes they took their disagreements to the press. It was no secret that Bryant found O'Neal frustrating, especially when it came to the off-season. Bryant worked hard. O'Neal preferred to get in shape during the season itself, an attitude that Bryant disagreed with.

Bryant and O'Neal often disagreed with one another as players. Years later, though, Bryant likened their relationship to that of brothers, sometimes troublesome but overall affectionate.

Though their feud was no secret, neither was one other thing: they managed to put it aside during games. The two of them led the Lakers to three consecutive championships between 2000 and 2002—the second three-peat in the history of the NBA. In the 2001

SHAQ ATTACK

Shaquille Rashaun O'Neal was born on March 6, 1972, in Newark, New Jersey. When Shaq's high school team in San Antonio, Texas, won the state championship, college scouts paid attention. In college at Louisiana State University (LSU), he didn't take long to become known as one of the nation's best players. In 1992 at the **NBA draft**, he was the Orlando Magic's first pick before he graduated from LSU, which he did in 2000.

As 1992–1993 Rookie of the Year, he boosted the Magic's win record by twenty wins to 41–41. His success was due in no small part to his size and strength: he stood seven feet, one inch (2.16 meters) tall and weighed 315 pounds (143 kilograms), making him an unstoppable offensive end. In 1996, he helped the US Olympic basketball team to a gold medal and joined the LA Lakers. He and Kobe Bryant shared the spotlight as superstars. In 1999–2000, he earned the league's Most Valuable Player (MVP) honor.

A series of trades sent him to the Miami Heat in 2004, the Phoenix Suns in 2008, the Cleveland Cavaliers in 2009, and the Boston Celtics in 2010. An Achilles tendon injury convinced him to retire after the 2010–2011 season. With 28,596 points, he became the seventh highest scorer in **NBA** history. In 2016, the Naismith Memorial Basketball Hall of Fame welcomed him into their ranks.

play-offs, the Lakers won a record fifteen out of sixteen games. The bickering and dissent between the O'Neal and Bryant would not end anytime soon, and in 2004 it led to Shaquille O'Neal being traded to the Miami Heat. But in the meantime, the Lakers worked together effectively.

Bryant towers over Disney's Goofy character during a family visit to Disneyland in 2010, before the birth of his youngest daughter in 2016.

In later years, both Bryant and O'Neal downplayed stories of their animosity. Bryant said they were like brothers, and he held no ill will against O'Neal. O'Neal shared that sentiment at the unveiling of his statue outside the Lakers' stadium in Los Angeles. "We pushed each other, we had our battles, we had our times. But we always had respect for each other, and we were able to win three championships."

PERSONAL MATTERS

For a brief time in the late 1990s and in 2000, Kobe Bryant flirted with the idea of a career alongside basketball: that of rap singer. After all, his teammate Shaquille O'Neal put out four albums in the 1990s, and they achieved a measure of success: his album *Shaq Diesel* sold 864,000 copies, making it a platinum seller. Kobe's album, called *Visions*, was set to debut in spring 2000. A single from the album, called "K.O.B.E.," was released beforehand to some excitement since it also featured supermodel Tyra Banks. But the single didn't go over well, and the record company, Sony, decided to pull the plug on the album release.

ABOUT THE LOS ANGELES LAKERS

In 1946, a team called the Detroit Gems was founded. It played in the National Basketball League (NBL) for one year before moving to Minneapolis, Minnesota, where its name was changed to the Lakers, since the team was now in Minnesota, the "Land of Ten Thousand Lakes." The Lakers snagged George Mikan that same year, a popular center. During the 1948–1949 season, the Lakers joined the BAA and won the final championship. In 1949, the BAA was absorbed into the NBA. Laker players Jim Pollard, Slater Martin, Vern Mikkelsen, and Clyde Lovellette seized four of the first five titles.

When Mikan retired in 1946, game attendance suffered. The team moved to Los Angeles prior to the 1960–1961 season. During the 1971–1972 season, Lakers stars Jerry West, Gail Goodrich, and Wilt Chamberlain set records for a thirty-three-game winning streak, the longest in NBA history.

Magic Johnson came aboard the team during the 1979 NBA draft. He teamed with Kareem Abdul-Jabbar and James Worthy to take five championships in 1980, 1982, 1985, 1987, and 1988. When Abdul-Jabbar retired in 1989 and Johnson followed him in 1991, the Lakers declined, making the play-offs most of the time but failing to advance to the finals.

During the 1999–2000 season, coach Phil Jackson took the helm as Shaquille O'Neal and Kobe Bryant dominated the team. After three consecutive titles, O'Neal was traded in 2004 and the team regrouped under Bryant and achieved notable successes like routing the Orlando Magic in five games for the championship. In 2009–2010, the Lakers defeated the Boston Celtics in a seven-game series. The team entered a period of plummeting performances, which led to Magic Johnson taking over as the team's president of basketball operations after the 2015–2016 season.

Bryant's rap career did have an unexpected legacy, though. While filming a music video in 1999, he met seventeen-year-old background dancer Vanessa Laine. The two began dating and married in 2001.

The Bryants went on to have three daughters: Natalia Diamante Bryant, born January 19, 2003; Gianna Maria-Onore Bryant, born May 1, 2006; and Bianka Bella Bryant, born December 5, 2016.

In 2003, while Bryant was in Colorado for knee surgery, he was arrested and charged with sexual assault of a ski resort employee. The criminal charge was later dropped when the woman refused to testify. Later, the woman filed a civil court case against Bryant. The case was settled out of court. It included a public apology to his accuser. During the apology, which he gave with his wife at his side, Bryant admitted to having an affair with the woman but denied raping her. The court case did not end in jail for Bryant, but it did stain his reputation, which had been scandal free until then.

CHAPTER FOUR

THE BLACK MAMBA

Kobe Bryant has collected a number of nicknames over the course of his career. Most of them have come courtesy of others, from sports commentators to coaches and other players. They include KB-24 (his initials and his jersey number from 2006 onward), the 8th Wonder of the World, Mr. 81, Kobe Wan Kenobi, Lord of the Rings (championship rings, that is), and Ocho (Spanish for the number 8, his initial jersey number). But there's one nickname that Bryant gave himself: the Black Mamba. In Quentin Tarantino's movie *Kill Bill*, Black Mamba is an assassin named after an aggressive, agile, and deadly snake. Bryant read up on the snake. He was impressed. He recalled, "This is a perfect description of how I would want my game to be."

The nickname was more than just a passing fancy. Instead, it was a sort of alter ego he created to triumph over his struggles on court and off court. When he was on the court as the Black Mamba, he could channel his energy constructively. He told Business Insider, "I had all this frustration that I just needed to let out. It was an avalanche, man. There was nothing that was going to get in the way. There was nothing that was going to stop me."

His ferocity, he explained, was not so much about his opponents as "the battle that was going on within [himself]."

Nike even teamed up with Bryant and director Robert Rodriguez to make a shoe commercial that focused on the Black Mamba character who saves a hostage—a little dog.

BREAKING RECORDS

After Shaq left the Lakers in 2004, the Lakers struggled without his talents. Kobe rallied, stepping into the gap Shaq left and challenging himself to come out of his shell toward his teammates.

He made an effort to get to know them, to loosen up, and in doing so became the Lakers' sole leader. He led the league in scoring in both the 2005–2006 and 2006–2007 seasons. He was at the top of his game, famously scoring a career-high 81 points against the Toronto Raptors in

Bryant goes for the basket during a game against the Toronto Raptors in November 2006. Earlier that year, he had reached his career-high score playing against the same team.

January 2006, the second-most points scored since Wilt Chamberlain's 100-point game in 1962.

In 2008, he won his first MVP award. When NBA commissioner David Stern handed over Bryant's award, he said, "You've helped mold (the Lakers) into a championship contender, and when we didn't think you could get any better, you did. There have been many MVP performances this season. But as it's been said, there can be only one, and that one is Kobe Bryant."

Bryant went on to prove that Stern's words still applied to him when he earned gold medals on the 2008 and 2012 US Olympic teams. The year 2009 brought his fourth NBA title when the Lakers defeated the Orlando Magic in the finals. During the series, he averaged 32.4 points per game and snagged another MVP honor.

In the Lakers game against the Timberwolves on December 14, 2014, Bryant passed Michael Jordan's all-time free throw record.

In 2009–2010, he charged on, earning another MVP when the Lakers defeated the Boston Celtics in a seven-game series. During the following two seasons the Lakers won division titles but lost out during the second round of both postseasons. In December 2014, he passed up childhood icon Michael Jordan for third place on the NBA all-time scoring list.

COULD ANYTHING STOP BRYANT?

Injuries could. They began to pile up. A torn Achilles tendon in April 2013 sidelined him for the 2012–2013 season, as did a fractured knee six games

BASKETBALL INJURIES

Being an elite athlete comes with its fair share of rewards: fame, money, and more. It also comes with risks, such as injuries related to the game. In basketball, there are a number of common injuries that can keep players out of the game entirely or just hamper their performance. These include ankle sprains, which often occur when the player moves from side to side quickly or when a player jumps and lands on another's foot. After a player has injured an ankle once from a sprain, he or she is at increased risk for another sprain in the future. Knee ligament injuries involve everything from mild sprains to complete tears. If the ligament is torn, surgery is often necessary, as is a long rehab program.

Jumper's knee refers to an injury of the tendon that connects the kneecap to the lower leg. Because this tendon is put under stress due to repetitive jumping and sprinting, it can become inflamed or cause a longer-lasting injury. Rest, stretches, anti-inflammatory medicine, and a strength program are the best treatments.

The Achilles tendon is also under a great deal of stress in basketball. An overuse injury can develop, as can the rupturing of a tendon. If the tendon ruptures the athlete will need to stop playing for the rest of the season.

Finally, concussions are also a risk when players bang heads or fall and strike the floor. Generally, the treatment includes rest and a slow return to play.

into the 2013–2014 season. An unwelcome three-peat occurred in the 2014–2015 season when he suffered a torn rotator cuff and was unable to finish the season. He came back ready to go in the 2015–2016 season, but not for long. He struggled against his younger teammates and admitted to the Players' Tribune website: "My heart can take the pounding. My mind can handle the grind but my body knows it's time to say goodbye."

Surrounded by the media, Bryant speaks to the crowd at his final game on April 13, 2016, at the Staples Center in Los Angeles, California.

The time had come for Bryant to retire from the game he loved so much. NBA commissioner Adam Silver issued a statement that said, "With 17 NBA All-Star selections, an NBA MVP, five NBA championships with the Lakers, two Olympic gold medals and a relentless work ethic, Kobe Bryant is one of the greatest players in the history of our game."

Bryant played his last game on April 13, 2016, against the Utah Jazz, where he scored 60 points—the sixth time he had done that—and led the Lakers to one final win. Bryant had set the record for playing the most seasons with one franchise, twenty years with the LA Lakers. At his final game, he told the crowd, "I can't believe how fast 20 years went by."

CHAPTER FIVE

THE ROAD AHEAD

Kobe Bryant may have retired from basketball in 2016, but that didn't mean he was done with the sport entirely. At only thirty-eight years of age, he had a lot of other endeavors to take on. They would take the form of charity work, serving on Olympic commissions, producing children's media, and more.

HOMECOMING

The best known of Bryant's charities is the one he and his wife set up in 2006. The Kobe and Vanessa Bryant Family Foundation (KVBFF) works to improve the lives of youth and families in need, both at home and across the world. Encouraging young people to stay active through sports is a big part of their mission. The foundation provides money and unique programs to bring awareness to good works that can result in stronger communities for all.

In 2007, he set up the Kobe Bryant Basketball Academy, which provides a summer camp where he mentors and trains athletes from eight to eighteen years of age and funds scholarships for minority college students. Also in 2007, Bryant became the ambassador for After-School All-Stars, a children's charity that serves seventy-three thousand inner-city kids with after-school programs that nurture their minds, bodies, and spirits.

In 2009, Bryant established the Kobe Bryant China Fund after his time in China during the 2008 Olympics. The fund cooperates with the Chinese government to raise money for the promotion of health and education in China. Bryant is extremely popular in China. One piece of evidence for that is the large statue of him in the province of Guangzhou outside of a museum.

Ending homelessness is a special concern of Bryant's. He saw homeless people walking the streets outside the stadiums where he played basketball games, but he didn't think much about it until he learned just how many people are affected. A 2011 report from the Los Angeles Homeless Services Authority numbers the homeless in Los Angeles County as more than fifty thousand at any given time. Bryant said, "It puts things into perspective. At the end of the day there's only so many interviews you can do and stories you can write. You have to do something that carries more weight and has more significance and purpose to it."

Bryant poses with members of the Kobe Basketball Academy at Loyola Marymount University in Los Angeles, California.

Bryant and his wife, Vanessa, have toured facilities such as a center for homeless youth in Hollywood to bring awareness to the problem and to deliver funds from the KVBFF to help with programs. Bryant said, "This isn't a popular topic or a popular issue. It's one where you have to get your hands dirty a little bit. It's not something celebrities easily rally around but this is something that we wanted to change."

And that's not the extent of Bryant's support for charities. He volunteers for United Way of Greater Los Angeles, Make-A-Wish Foundation, NBA Cares, and the Boys & Girls Clubs of America.

SPOTLIGHT ON BRYANT'S FOUNDATION

The Kobe and Vanessa Bryant Family Foundation supports a number of programs throughout the Los Angeles area. These include Mamba FC, a youth soccer club in Orange County that emphasizes leadership and teamwork, and My Friend's Place, a Hollywood-based effort that serves homeless youth. Vanessa Bryant often visits the young parents there. Step Up on Second, located in Santa Monica, helps the homeless locate permanent housing. Bryant regularly acts as the United Way's honorary cochair for the HomeWalk, which draws more than ten thousand people annually to raise money for homeless services.

During a visit to Skid Row, an impoverished section of downtown Los Angeles, in 2012, Bryant said, "The feeling you get when you are walking in Skid Row…it's like the people are just forgotten by society."

Bryant does what he can to remember the homeless and help them live better lives. The foundation's website lists sobering statistics about homelessness:

- 25 percent of the homeless are aged seventeen and younger
- the average minor on the streets has been homeless for nearly three years
- 69 percent of homeless young people have suffered child abuse

On an international level, Bryant continues his interest in China. KVBFF helps students tour China in coordination with the UCLA

Brady poses with fans during the 2013 Tom Brady Football Challenge in Hyannis Port, Massachusetts.

autism, among other conditions. Brady helps the organization raise money through an annual charity football game and participates in a yearly charity walk, run, and ride called the Best Buddies Challenge: Hyannis Port.

Brady, known as the group's global ambassador, says, "Best Buddies is a fantastic organization with a great message to spread, and I am so proud to support their work. I hope my role as Honorary Co-Chair will continue to bring attention to the organization's mission of friendship and inclusion for people with intellectual and developmental disabilities across the world."

Brady began volunteering to help the organization in 2001. Since then, the organization credited him with helping to raise more than forty million dollars. Brady called his work with Best Buddies "one of my greatest honors."

BECOME A BEST BUDDY

Best Buddies was founded in 1989 by Anthony K. Shriver, who is a nephew of President John F. Kennedy and Senators Robert F. Kennedy and Ted Kennedy. Best Buddies, a nonprofit organization, first came into being when Shriver inspired fellow college students to help IDD individuals in a hands-on way. The original chapter grew to include more than 2,300 middle school, high school, and college chapters worldwide. The organization's eight programs (Middle Schools, High Schools, Colleges, Citizens, e-Buddies®, Jobs, Ambassadors, and Promoters) have made positive changes in more than 1.1 million people in the United States and around the world. Volunteers benefit people with IDD by forming friendships with them, helping them find work, and assisting them to live independently.

TB12: THE COMPANY AND FOUNDATION

Brady's 2017 book isn't the only TB12 product. The TB12 website sells a range of products approved by Brady. They include protein powders, bars, and snacks, workout gear like weighted vests and medicine balls, apparel, and even the Brain HQ, which includes apps to exercise and improve memory and focus.

Brady also founded the TB12 Foundation, which is dedicated to: "maximizing the health, well-being, and athletic potential of elite young American amateur athletes by providing free access to the best available post-injury rehabilitation and performance enhancement services." The foundation accomplishes this through one-on-one sessions with athletes and educational programs to schools that lack such resources. Brady established it because he wanted to encourage athletes to obtain care that goes beyond just treating symptoms—quick fixes—instead of addressing underlying injury causes. It conducts both one-on-one sessions and educational events with groups. So far, more than 740 sessions have been provided to athletes at a market cost of nearly $150,000.

Brady's charitable work doesn't stop there, though. He also works to support and donate to the Boys & Girls Club, the Rodman Ride for Kids, an athletic fundraiser to earn money for supporting at-risk kids, the Santa Monica Catholic Community, charities run by his football friends, and his children's private school. After he won his second MVP, Brady donated a Cadillac to his old high school for a raffle. It brought the school $375,000.

RETIREMENT?

Brady has already accomplished more than most pro football players could ever dream of accomplishing. But what is next for him? More playing time? Or retirement? In March 2017, New England Patriots owner Robert Kraft reported that Brady wanted to continue to play. In fact, Kraft said that, "As recently as two or three days ago, he assured me that he'd be willing to play another six or seven years."

During an interview with SiriusXM NFL Radio, Brady admitted that his wife wants him to retire. SiriusXM NFL Radio reported on its Twitter account that he said: "If it was up to my wife she'd have me retire today, she told me that last night...I said too bad, babe."

Tom Brady, wife, Gisele Bündchen, and sons, Jack and Benjamin, enjoy a family day out during a 2013 visit to Disneyland.

Brady is triumphant during 2017's AFC Championship Game, pitting the New England Patriots against the Pittsburgh Steelers.

Brady has said that he would prefer to play until his mid-forties. He told Peter King from The MMQB that he would make a decision then. "If I'm still feeling like I'm feeling today, who knows?"

Clearly, Brady is optimistic about his future playing time. But history does not lie, and he knows that he's pushing the limit of his abilities and age. Though he reported that he is having a lot of fun, things can change in the blink of an eye.

A USA Today feature put it bluntly. "He's living on borrowed time as it is. Who's 40 in the NFL? Almost no one, that's who."

Traditionally, NFL players retire by their late thirties. The average career length for an NFL player is 3.3 years, according to the NFL Players Association. However, as more research about the long-term impact of chronic traumatic encephalopathy (CTE), a progressive disease of the brain that results from repeated blows to the head, some are electing to retire earlier. A Boston University study reports that CTE appeared in the brains of an astounding ninety of ninety-four former NFL players. Another study indicates that young athletes who play football before the age of twelve can suffer brain problems in later life.

Clearly, Brady has not allowed sobering statistics like these to deter him from playing the game he loves. And he's proved over the years that he's willing to take whatever actions are physically possible to achieve the unexpected. Because of that, he's a good candidate to defy the odds. After all, he's made a career of doing it already.

FACT SHEET

Born

August 3, 1977, in San Mateo, California

Height

6 feet 4 inches (1.93 m)

Weight

225 pounds (102 kg)

Education

High School—Junipero Serra High School in San Mateo, California; College—University of Michigan

Position

Quarterback

Accomplishments

- Five-time NFL Super Bowl champion
- Two-time MVP award recipient
- Twelve-time Pro Bowl player
- NFL Comeback Player of the Year

- Holds the record for most passing yards in one year: 5,235 (2011)
- Holds record for most touchdowns in one year: 50 (2007)

2017 statistics

- Rating: 102.8
- Yards: 4,577
- Interception: 8
- Touchdowns: 32

Charity work

Best Buddies International
TB12 Foundation

Books

The TB12 Method: How to Achieve a Lifetime of Sustained Peak Performance

TIMELINE

1977: On August 3, Tom Brady is born in San Mateo, California.

1995: Brady attends the University of Michigan and joins their team, the Wolverines.

1998: Brady becomes the Wolverines' starting quarterback.
Brady and the Wolverines win the Citrus Bowl against Arkansas.

1999: Brady and the Wolverines win the Orange Bowl.

2000: The New England Patriots draft Tom Brady in the sixth round.

2001: Brady takes over as the starting quarterback in the third game of the season.

2002: On February 3, the Patriots appear in Super Bowl XXXVI.
Brady is named Super Bowl MVP.

2004: Brady and the Patriots win Super Bowl XXXVIII.
Brady is named Super Bowl MVP.

2005: Brady and the Patriots triumph at Super Bowl XXXIX.

2007: The Patriots accomplish the first 16–0 regular season in NFL history.
Brady's son John Moynahan is born.
Brady is named MVP for the season.

2008: The Patriots lose Super Bowl XLII to the New York Giants.

2009: Brady marries Gisele Bündchen; son Benjamin is born.

2010: Brady wins the season MVP award.

2012: The Patriots lose Super Bowl XLVI to the New York Giants.
Brady's daughter Vivian is born.

2015: The Patriots win Super Bowl XLIX over the Seattle Seahawks.
Brady is named Super Bowl MVP.

2016: Brady is suspended for four games due to Deflategate ruling.

2017: The Patriots win the Super Bowl against the Atlanta Falcons.
Brady releases his first book.
Brady is named Super Bowl MVP.

2018: The Patriots lose Super Bowl LII to the Philadelphia Eagles.

GLOSSARY

appendectomy Surgery to remove a person's appendix.

devolve To go from a high level to a lesser level over time.

draft To pick a sports player to join a team.

durability The state of being able to last a long time.

feat An accomplishment.

idolized Loved or admired to a great degree.

ligament A tough band of tissue that holds bones and organs in place.

prognosis A prediction or forecast.

psychological Of or related to human thoughts and the mind.

quarterback A football player who directs plays against the other team.

rehabilitation Bringing back to a condition of health.

rupture To break or tear apart.

safety A defensive position in football; the safety, one of the defensive backs, lines up ten to fifteen yards in front of the scrimmage line.

snap The backward passing of the football from the scrimmage line.

tedious Boring or repetitious.

tenacity The state of holding fast to an action or belief.

tight end A player position on a football team that involves duties of both the offensive lineman and the wide receiver.

unanimously Complete agreement by all involved.

yardage A total number of yards.

FOR MORE INFORMATION

Boys & Girls Clubs of America
National Headquarters
1275 Peachtree Street NE
Atlanta, GA 30309-3506
(404) 487-5700
Website: http://www.bgca.org
Facebook: @bgca.clubs
Twitter and Instagram: @bgca_clubs
A network of clubs across the country whose mission is to help young
    people reach their potential as productive, caring, and responsible citi-
    zens. Sports programs are emphasized, as are other education, arts,
    and health and wellness programs.

Canadian Football League
50 Wellington Street East–3rd Floor
Toronto, ON M5E 1C8
Canada
(416) 322-9650
Website: https://www.cfl.ca
Facebook and Twitter: @CFL
Instagram: @cfl
A professional sports league that supports the highest level of Canadian
    football competition.

National Football League (NFL)
280 Park Avenue, 15th Floor
New York, NY 10017
(212) 450-2000
Website: https://www.nfl.com
Facebook and Twitter: @NFL

Instagram: @nfl

A professional American football league that consists of teams divided between the National Football Conference and the American Football Conference. The website and other social media pages provide extensive information on games, players, and associated businesses.

USA Football
45 N. Pennsylvania Street, Suite 700
Indianapolis, IN 46204
(877) 536-6822
Website: https://www.usafootball.com
Facebook and Twitter: @usafootball
Instagram: @usa_football

USA Football is an organization that works to make football better and safer by supporting coach and player improvement. USA Football is both a member and national governing body of the US Olympic Committee.

FOR FURTHER READING

Anastacio, Dina. *What Is the Super Bowl?* New York, NY: Penguin Workshop, 2015.

Barrington, Richard. *Tom Brady: Super Bowl Champion.* New York, NY: Rosen Publishing, 2016.

Brady, Tom. *The TB12 Method: How to Achieve a Lifetime of Sustained Peak Performance.* New York, NY: Simon & Schuster, 2017.

Braun, Eric. *Tom Brady.* Minneapolis, MN: Lerner Publications, 2017.

Challen, Paul. *What Does a Quarterback Do?* New York, NY: Rosen Publishing, 2015.

Curcio, Anthony. *New England Patriots 2017 Super Bowl Champions: The Ultimate Football Coloring, Activity and Stats Book for Adults and Kids.* CreateSpace, 2017.

Doeden, Matt. *The Super Bowl: Chasing Football Immortality.* Minneapolis, MN: Millbrook Press, 2017.

Nagelhout, Ryan. *Tom Brady (Today's Great Quarterbacks).* Gareth Stevens Publishing, 2014.

Nagelhout, Ryan. *The Science of Football.* New York, NY: Rosen Publishing, 2015.

Stewart, Mark. *The Michigan Wolverines.* Chicago, IL: Norwood House Press, 2009.

Van Pelt, Don, and Brian Wingate. *An Insider's Guide to Football.* New York, NY: Rosen Publishing, 2015.

BIBLIOGRAPHY

AP. "FAN GUIDE: A Look at Common Football Injuries." USA Today, September 17, 2015. https://www.usatoday.com/story/sports /nfl/2015/09/17/fan-guide-a-look-at-common-football-injuries/32542841.

Best Buddies. "Anthony K. Shriver, Founder and Chairman." Retrieved October 4, 2017. https://www.bestbuddies.org/about-us /anthony-k-shriver.

Best Buddies. "Join Tom Brady & Challenge Yourself to Change Lives at the 18th Annual Best Buddies Challenge: Hyannis Port Presented by Pepsi-Cola, Shaw's Foundation and Star Market Foundation." May 31, 2017. https://www.bestbuddies.org/blog/2017/06/06/18th-annual-best -buddies-challenge-hyannis-port-presented-pepsi-cola-shaws -foundation-star-market-foundation-raises-record-breaking-6 -million-people-intellectual-develo.

Biography. "Tom Brady." February 6, 2017. http://www.biography.com /people/tom-brady-259541.

Bishop, Greg. "The Other Side of Brady." SI.com, December 12, 2014. https://www.si.com/2014/12/12/tom-brady-off-field-former-teammates.

Brady, Tom. *The TB12 Method: How to Achieve a Lifetime of Sustained Peak Performance.* New York, NY: Simon & Schuster, 2017.

Brennan, Christine. "Happy 40th Birthday to Tom Brady: Retirement Is Closer Than You Think." USA Today, August 3, 2017. https://www .usatoday.com/story/sports/columnist/brennan/2017/08/03 /tom-bradys-40th-birthday-why-its-time-him-retire/534446001.

BU School of Medicine. "Study Suggests Link between Youth Football and Later-Life Emotional, Behavioral and Cognitive Impairments." BU Research CET Center, September 19, 2017. https://www.bumc. bu.edu/busm/2017/09/19/study-suggests-link-between-youth -football-and-later-life-emotional-behavioral-and-cognitive-impairments.

CBS News. "Look Inside the Company Creating the Super Bowl Rings." February 6, 2016. https://www.cbsnews.com/news

/super-bowl-2016-championship-rings-look-inside-designer
-company-jostens.

Cimini, Rich. "Story of Boy Named Tom Brady." *New York Daily News*, January 25, 2008. http://www.nydailynews.com/sports/football/giants /story-boy-named-tom-brady-article-1.341686.

Cole, Mike. "Tom Brady Says Gisele Wishes He Would Retire, but He's Not Going Anywhere." NESN, February 6, 2017. https://nesn .com/2017/02/tom-brady-says-gisele-wishes-he-would-retire-but -hes-not-going-anywhere.

Curran, Tom E. "Tom Brady Sr.: 'We're Not Gonna Rage.'" NBC Sports Boston, February 4, 2016. http://www.nbcsports.com/boston /new-england-patriots/tom-brady-sr-%E2%80%98we%E2%80%99re -not-gonna-rage%E2%80%99.

Editors of Encyclopædia Britannica. "National Football League (NFL)." Britannica Library, September 9, 2017. https://www .britannica.com/topic/National-Football-League.

Editors of Encyclopaedia Britannica. "Tom Brady." Encyclopaedia Britannica Online, August 4, 2017. http://www.britannica.com /biography/Tom-Brady.

ESPN.com. "NFL History—Super Bowl Winners." Retrieved October 4, 2017. http://www.espn.com/nfl/superbowl/history/winners.

Fox Sports. "Why More NFL Players Will Retire Early Like Calvin Johnson." March 14, 2016. https://www.foxsports.com/nfl/story /nfl-cte-link-brain-disease-calvin-johnson-bj-raji-retirement -early-young-leaving-game-031416.

Good Celebrity. "Tom Brady Is an MVP On & Off the Football Field: A Complete Look at the Patriots QB's Charity Work." February 3, 2017. http://www.goodcelebrity.com/2017/02/03/tom-brady -mvp-off-football-field-complete-look-patriots-qbs-charity-work.

Hohler, Bob. "Tom Brady Gives Much to Best Buddies, but Has Taken Millions for His Own Charitable Trust." Boston Globe, April 22, 2017.

https://www.bostonglobe.com/sports/2017/04/22/tom-brady
-gives-much-best-buddies-but-takes-millions-for-his-personal-trust
/fX6A4ZqPaYAehmHllm9iLl/story.html.

Jenkins, Lee. "Self-Made Man." SI.com, January 31, 2008. https://www
.si.com/more-sports/2008/01/31/tombrady.

JockBio.com. "Tom Brady: Biography." Retrieved September 9, 2017.
http://www.jockbio.com/Bios/Brady_Tom/Brady_bio.html.

Kyed, Doug. "Tom Brady Vows 2017 Won't Be Final Season, Reveals
Intended Age of Retirement." NESN, February 15, 2017. https://
nesn.com/2017/02/tom-brady-vows-2017-wont-be-final-season
-reveals-intended-age-of-retirement.

Merrill, Elizabeth. "12 Things to Know about Tom Brady." ESPN,
February 1, 2012. http://www.espn.com/nfl/playoffs/2011/story
/_/id/7525476/tom-brady-12-things-not-known-new-england-star
-quarterback.

NFL.com. "NFL.com 2016 Media Kit." Retrieved October 4, 2017.
https://www.nfl.com/static/content/public/photo/2016
/08/09/0ap3000000682159.pdf.

Sargent, Hilary. "Meet the Chef Who Decides What Tom Brady Eats—
and What He Definitely Doesn't." Boston.com, January 4, 2016.
https://www.boston.com/sports/new-england-patriots/2016/01/04
/meet-the-chef-who-decides-what-tom-brady-eatsand-what-he
-definitely-doesnt.

Springer, Shira. "Brady Has Both ACL and MCL Tears." Boston.com,
September 11, 2008. http://archive.boston.com/sports
/articles/2008/09/11/brady_has_both_acl_and_mcl_tears.

TB12 Foundation. "About the Foundation." Retrieved October 5, 2017.
https://tb12foundation.com.

WWECenaManiaTV. "Super Bowl XXXVI—Tom Brady's Final Drive
(2002)." January 15, 2017. https://youtu.be/0WNBQmcPh24.

INDEX

ABOUT THE AUTHOR

Xina M. Uhl has written numerous educational books for young people as well as textbooks, teacher's guides, lessons, and assessment questions. She has tackled subjects including sports, history, biographies, technology, and health concerns. Her parents saw the name Xina on a cheerleader's jersey when watching a football game and decided to give her that name. Her blog details her publications as well as interesting facts and the occasional cat picture.

PHOTO CREDITS